BOOK FORMATTING TIPS

A Guide for Self-Publishing Authors

By:

V. Karen McMahon

TABLE OF CONTENTS

FORMATTING TIPS
USING MICROSOFT WORD

Step-by-Step Instructions on
How to Format Your Own Book

FOREWORD

So if you have less hair today and seem to have to take a few more antacids than you did when you started trying to get your manuscript formatted for submittal, don't feel alone. The non-intuitive functions of Microsoft Word can do that to you! I've been editing and formatting for many years, and I remember well the day that Bill Gates murdered Word Perfect. There was a hard, painful transfer from Word Perfect to Microsoft Word, and to this day it is my opinion that Bill didn't even come close to the quality of Word Perfect. And every time Bill "upgrades" Word, it gets worse. Every command that you FINALLY learned which was not intuitive to begin with, is now gone. Even seasoned professionals struggle with the learning curve with each new "edition."

In my work with other writers, I've seen even more frustration than among those who had no choice and HAD to master it to survive in our jobs. They want to write, not spend their lives trying to master Microsoft Word. The problem comes for many authors when they hire someone to edit their manuscript, and assume—rightly or wrongly—that the editor will also fix all the formatting problems they've encountered. I've been approached by many authors who have already paid for editing and are begging for help to put their manuscript in a format that a publisher will accept, and they're always distraught because they had assumed that the editor would fix those issues as well.

Formatting can be every bit as time-consuming as editing—perhaps even more so—and therefore is not cheap. Plus you will find that most editors, even those who are good, quality editors, don't know how to do the formatting, either. So to avoid paying twice, as many of you have, why not master the program yourself? Sure, there are a million Microsoft tutorials out there and many have told me they took them and they were too technical and blew their minds so they gave up. So I got the idea of writing a SIMPLIFIED short tutorial to show you both visually and verbally how to do a lot of the things that I've been contacted to do that your editor couldn't or wouldn't do. I will attempt to show you with menu screens—and arrows along with written instructions—how to do everything you need to do to bring your book up to publishing standards (or as close as you can get to it without being a publishing professional doing typesetting).

This small tutorial is not intended to be a full Microsoft Word tutorial and will not include everything you can do in Microsoft Word. Rather, it is just intended to outline the steps you need to get your book ready to submit either as an ebook or to a publisher. You may or may not encounter some problems, depending on the contents of your book, that we haven't covered here. However, we will strive to cover all the main ingredients and hopefully help some authors through some serious angst so that they don't have to put their laptops in the trash can!

Another note here: This tutorial was created in Microsoft Word 2010 as that is what I have on my machine. And as usual, old Bill has made sure that there are some "differences" to justify having to buy each new issue. So if some of the menus across the top of your screen look a little different, don't panic. The instructions are pretty much the same and if you're working in an older version you may have to just use common sense to find the right menu and then follow the same instructions. Or, just go ahead and be a sheep like me and get 2010 but remember, there will be another learning curve in 2012 or 2013 or whenever, and I think it's about time for a new "release." But if you can get these fundamentals down now, new releases will not be as difficult.

SIZE YOUR DOCUMENT

The very FIRST thing you need to do when you start formatting your own book is to set the page size. This is vital, because if you let it default to an 8.5x11 size and then do all your formatting, somewhere along the line in this bizarre world of Microsoft Word—especially when you're working in a large document—you're going to run into a page numbering or other formatting problem. Start with the "Home" tab on your menu at the top, left-hand side of the page.

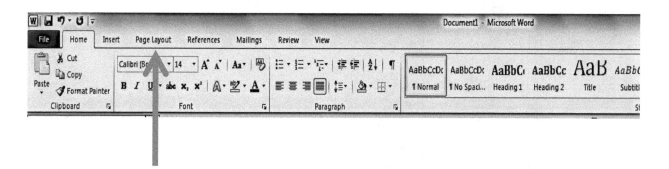

Go to "Page Layout"

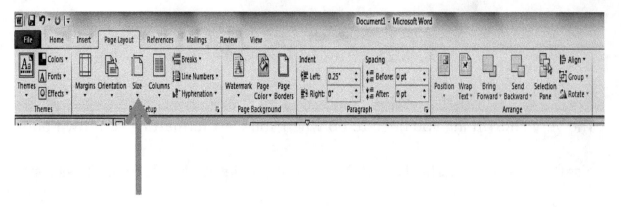

Choose "Size"

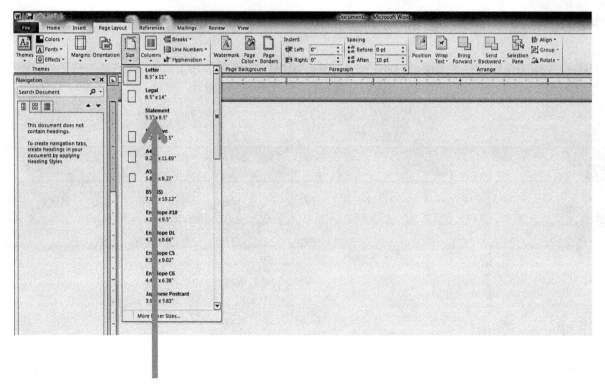

Under "Size", choose the size you want (The arrow points to Statement which is

size 5.5x8.5).

A book can be any size you want it to be (pretty much), but you won't see many at 8.5x11. Most novelists choose 6x9 or 5.5x8.5. When a publisher such as CreateSpace prints your book, it will be a lot cheaper if you pick the 5.5x8.5 size (Microsoft calls it "Statement" in their menu above) because that allows them to print two pages on every sheet. Literally, it can be half of the cost of a 6x9 which uses one whole sheet and it has to be cropped. So my recommendation is 5.5x8.5—your book will look thicker too because it will have a few more pages in that size but it will still considerably cheaper to print.

SET YOUR FONT

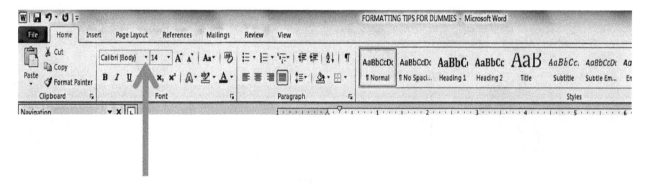

Next, choose the font you want to use. Almost all publishers will insist on a 12-point font and they particularly like Times New Roman for some reason, but I have never had them argue about any "straight" font—never use calligraphy or a fancy font except on title pages or the first inside page. Set your font now so that it will cover your entire document. Let it include your chapter headings and titles, and then at the end, go back and put "styles" onto JUST your headings. If you're already familiar with how to do styles, then of course do it as you go, but assigning styles and creating a template for your document may be more advanced than you wish to tackle, and it is not necessary. For now, set your font for the entire document the same, and you will see in the Table of Contents section below how to change the headings to your choice and create an automatic Table of Contents.

SET YOUR MARGINS

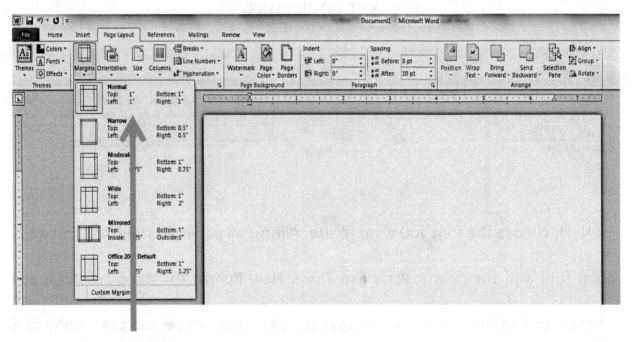

Most publishers require a margin of 1" all around.

Go to "Page Layout"

Click "Margins" and choose "Normal" option, 1" all around

AUTOMATIC INDENTS FOR PARAGRAPHS

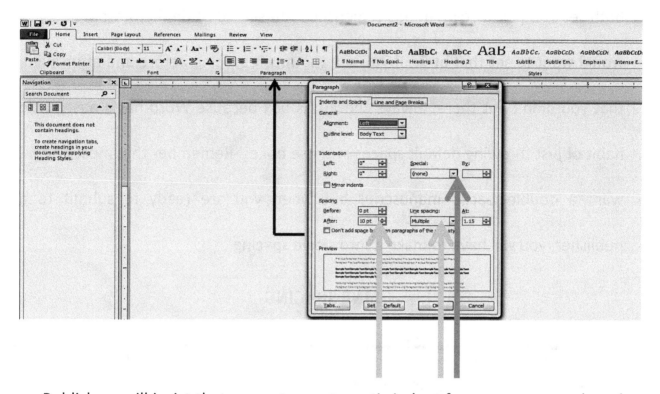

Publishers will insist that you set an automatic indent for every paragraph and will sometimes reject your document if it is not used. This is to ensure that all paragraphs are indented at the exact same spot, which may not hold when they convert it into the ebook format if you use the tab key to make your indents. Start with the "Home" menu and click on the "Paragraph" drop-down menu and then the "Indents and Spacing" tab. Choose an indention of .25 (far right arrow) and click "OK." From this point on, all paragraphs will be indented the same automatically, just by hitting your 'Enter' key to start a new paragraph. While you are in this box, go ahead and set your line spacing, i.e., double space (center arrow) or single space. Also—and this is a tricky one a lot of people forget to do or where it is—make sure there the spacing above and below the paragraph are both set at 0 (left arrow); in this screenshot you see 10 pt on the bottom and you would want to set that at 0. If you see too much spacing before and after a line that you didn't put there, always check this box because Word has a nasty little habit of just throwing default spaces in those boxes. Remember that most editors want a double-spaced manuscript but when you are ready to submit to a publisher, you will have to make it into single spacing.

LINE SPACING

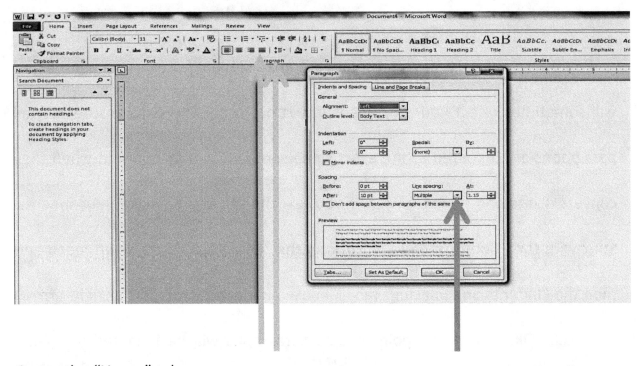

Go to the "Home" tab

Go to the "Paragraph" (center arrow)

Choose double space for your drafts; single for your finals (right arrow). Make sure the "above" and "below" (as discussed above) are both set to 0.

While you are here, set the line spacing to right justified (left arrow); all publishers require that you right justify the final copy of your manuscript.

YOUR COVER PAGE

Most authors don't worry about their cover until they have written their books, and this is fine. However, publishers require that you have a "title" page at the beginning of your "internal submission" that shows all of the information the cover would have and then some. For instance, compare my cover below and the inside cover sheet.

The outside covers, front and back, are submitted separately, so keep them in separate documents. Also, they will most likely have to be submitted in .jpeg or .tiff format, which Word—nasty old Word—will not do. I use PowerPoint to create my covers but any program that allows you to save it as a .jpeg or .tiff will suffice. If you do have a cover designed and it is inside your document, remove it (they will not accept artwork on the inside cover) and make it into its own file.

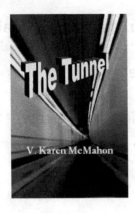

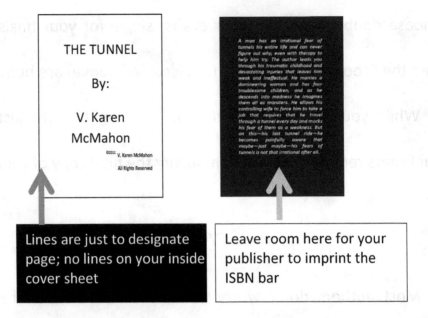

THE TUNNEL

By:

V. Karen
McMahon

©2011 V. Karen McMahon

All Rights Reserved

A man has an irrational fear of tunnels his entire life and can never figure out why, even with therapy to help him try. The author leads you through his traumatic childhood and devastating injuries that leaves him weak and ineffectual. He marries a domineering woman and has four troublesome children, and as he descends into madness he imagines them all as monsters. He allows his controlling wife to force him to take a job that requires that he travel through a tunnel every day and mocks his fear of them as a weakness. But on this—his last tunnel ride—he becomes painfully aware that maybe—just maybe—his fears of tunnels is not that irrational after all.

Lines are just to designate page; no lines on your inside cover sheet

Leave room here for your publisher to imprint the ISBN bar

SECTION BREAKS

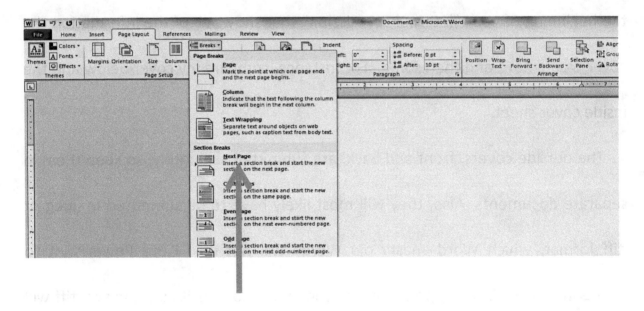

Go to the "Page Layout" menu – Click on "Breaks"

Click on "Section Break" – and then choose "Next Page"

Now we get to a toughie. Page breaks and section breaks are hard to learn to

use and are a bit complicated, and are the one that most of my clients have the most trouble with. To make life easy for yourself I suggest that you put a "Next-Page" section break at the end of EVERY section until you get to the first page that you want to denote as page 1. Sections include: 1) inside cover sheet; 2) pages for Table of Contents if you plan on having one; 3) acknowledgement or dedication pages, etc. That way you will be able to go back and remove page numbers from the preliminary pages that you do not want numbers on, or you can use a different number on some of the pages without it affecting page 1 and beyond. Once you get that mastered, you can type hundreds of pages and the numbers will be consecutive. When using section breaks, ALWAYS use "Next Page" and NEVER EVER use a continuous page break because it causes many other issues that are too complicated and unnecessary to go into here for our purposes.

Unless you just want to learn all about page and section breaks (which is not covered in this tutorial), don't worry about learning the many different uses of page vs section breaks, and continuous vs next page. If you use "Next Page" under "Section Break" for each section, then within that section you can change your page numbers and format that section differently from the rest AS LONG as you remember to tell it to DISCONNECT from the previous section (we talk about that in the page number section below). For the purposes of a novel, you will probably only need to have different page numbers and not find a need for other options.

PAGE NUMBERING

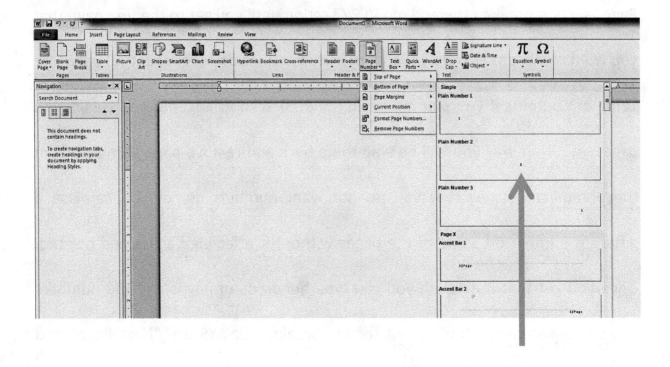

Double-click inside the footer section (just somewhere near the bottom will bring up the footer box) of your page.

Go to the "Insert" tab

Go to "Page Numbers" and click on the drop-down arrow

Most publishers require that the page number be bottom/center with no words or lines (second option, see arrow). When you are selecting the page number format here, be sure that you are below your section break command so that it will not put numbers in the previous sections. See example below:

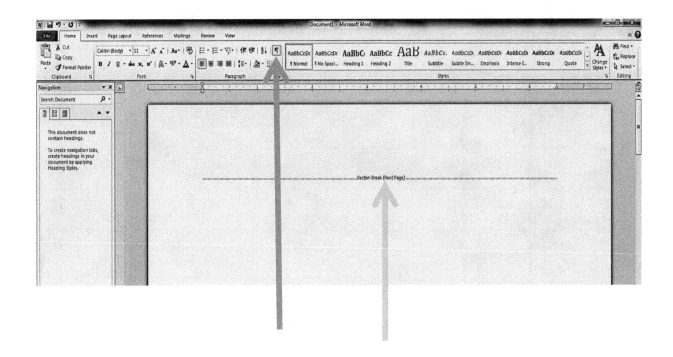

Turn on the paragraph symbol (left arrow) to show you where the section break is. Notice in the body, you will see the line saying "Section Break Next Page" (right arrow). This will disappear when you turn the paragraph sign off again, but make sure your cursor is below this line before you start inserting page numbers. If you notice that the page numbers are in the previous section, you can go to that section and change them, but BEFORE you do, make sure that you have deselected the option of connecting the page numbers to the previous sections. Always deselect this, even though it may be the first section.

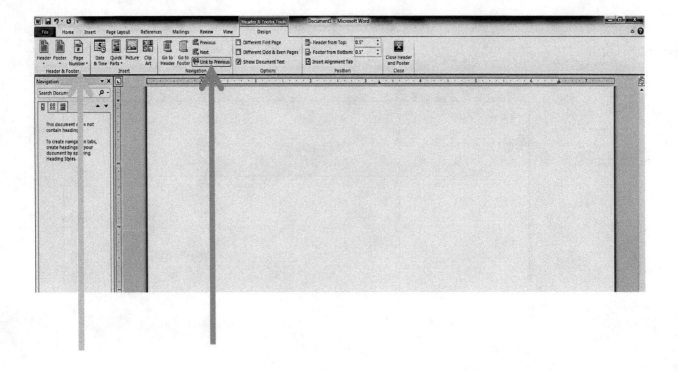

Double-click in the footer. If the "Link to Previous" button is highlighted (the default), click on it to turn it off. If it gives you the option to say "Yes" or "No", always choose "No." Put in your page number by clicking on the drop-down arrow by the "Page Number" icon (left arrow). For the preliminary sections, choose the roman numeral formatting and tell it to start with i. Then go to the footer of the next section, again deselect "Link to Previous", choose regular numbering and again tell it to start with 1. Each time you give these commands, you need to make sure you are working in the footer below the section break mark. Your document should be numbered correctly from this point on.

JUST A PRETTY

While I tried not to get any fancier here than you absolutely needed for your book, I thought I'd throw in one small "pretty" for your book. I changed the font here for the first letter only, just to show that it can be different. If you like drop caps (I think they look so professional and I like to use them), here's how to do it:

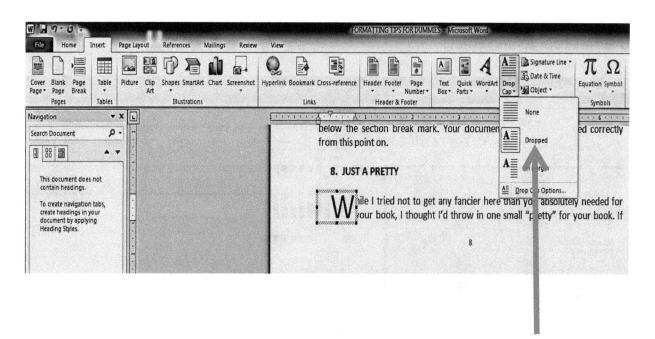

Highlight the first letter in your paragraph. Only use this at the very beginning of each chapter, not each paragraph – that would be serious overkill.

Go to the "Insert" tab

Click on the "Drop Cap" drop-down arrow and choose the 2nd option (for the one you see here—you can test the options and see which one you like best). Under that same tab, you can set the size of the first letter to take up as many lines as you like; the one you see is 3 lines (click on "Drop Cap Options" for this option). You can also change the font for that one letter and make it different from the rest of the paragraph; just use the regular font tab to make this change.

When you choose the drop cap, it will look as it does above, without color. If you wish to add color (remember now, most likely the inside of your book will be printed in black and white so preferably choose a black box with a white font), use this tool to add color:

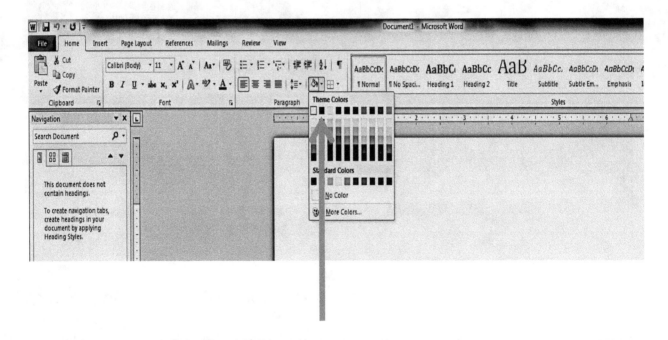

And it should look like the sample below; the letter will automatically change to a white font if you use black in the box. I didn't change the font here so that you can see how it looks either way.

14

While I have tried not to get any fancier here than you absolutely needed for your book, I thought I'd throw in one small....[**HINT**: always do your drop cap actions while single spaced; otherwise the black box will be too big for the letter that's in it].

NOW WRITE

Now write your book and don't worry about formatting anymore until you've gotten it done! There is one final step to do if you wish your book to have a Table of Contents. But NEVER do that until you've not only finished it, but had it edited. When you are sure you're ready to submit your book, then and only then do you want to bother with a TOC—although they can be updated (mentioned a little later on). When you are ready to do the TOC, an easy way is to go back and format your headings in the font and size you want, and then mark them for a TOC. Highlight the Chapter and Title:

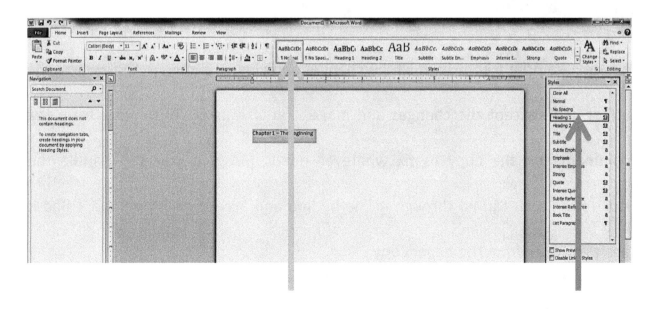

Go to the "Home" tab

Choose "Heading 1" (left arrow)

If this particular menu doesn't show on your version of Word, then go to the second arrow (right) – Click on the drop-down arrow at the bottom right of the "Styles" block (just below the "Change Styles" icon) to get your Styles menu to appear (right arrow). Make sure you are selecting the drop-down arrow at the bottom of the box, not the drop-down arrow for the "Change Styles" icon. Choose Heading 1 there. If you have subtitles, then follow the same procedure with those and choose a different style. Remember, however, that to use the default TOC option, which is by far the easiest (and is required by some publishers), you need to use Heading 1, Heading 2, or Heading 3 to get it to automatically appear.

TRACK CHANGES

If you receive a document back from an editor with track changes showing, my advice is to print a copy with all the changes showing, and then In the version the editor sent, accept the changes and make it your master. Then work from the comments on the copy to fix whatever needs fixing. If you can handle the frustration, you can go through it line by line and accept each one, but I find it easier to work from the paper copy.

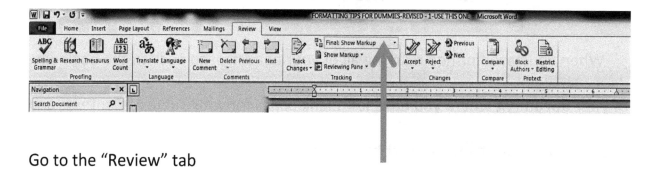

Go to the "Review" tab

Click on the "Final: Show Markup" drop-down menu

Click "Final"

The tracking marks will be hidden and you will only see your clean document as it would look with all of the editor's changes accepted. To be truly safe, once you see the clean copy, make yourself a new copy of the document, and specify in your title that it is the edited copy. Also, a good rule of thumb is, once you turn the document over to the editor, do not edit it yourself or make changes in it until you get it back. You don't want to have multiple copies of it floating around; it's a lot easier than you think to suddenly find yourself working in the wrong copy and lots of duplication and wasted time occurs.

CREATING THE TABLE OF CONTENTS

When you have finished marking all of your headings, go back to the beginning of your document where you have left blank pages for your Table of Contents and put your cursor at the top of that blank page.

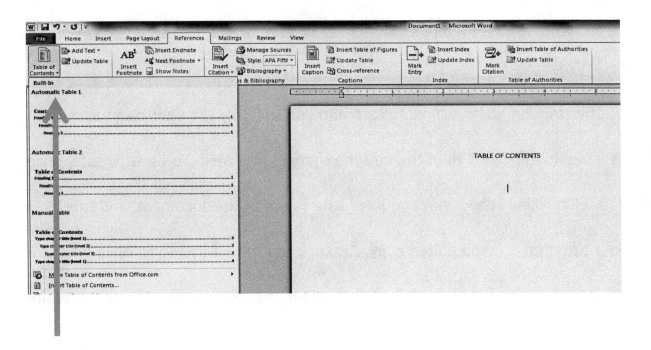

Go to the "References" tab

Click on the "Table of Contents" drop-down arrow (see arrow)

Click on the style of TOC you want

You may have to play around with this a little to find the best TOC for your book, depending on whether or not you have subtitles. The automatic one works as long as you have only used Headings 1, Heading 2 or Heading 3 styles. When your TOC is finished, if it is working correctly, you should be able to click or

CTRL/click on any line, and it will take you to that chapter in your book. You can update the TOC simply by right clicking somewhere in the TOC and telling it to update. It will give you the option of updating the entire TOC (not necessary unless you've changed a Chapter title), or page numbers only. It most instances, updating page numbers only is all you will need.

MAKING A PDF OF YOUR BOOK

Most publishers, especially for ebooks, will require a pdf of the interior of your book. This is extremely simple in Microsoft Word now (if you have a later version, that is; some of the older versions did not make it easy to do a pdf).

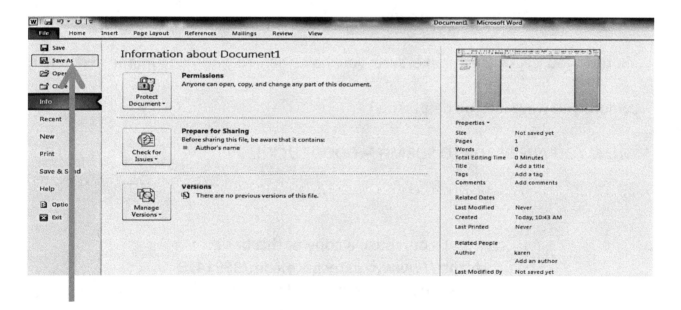

Go to the "File" then "Save As" tab (arrow) and get drop-down menu (see below)

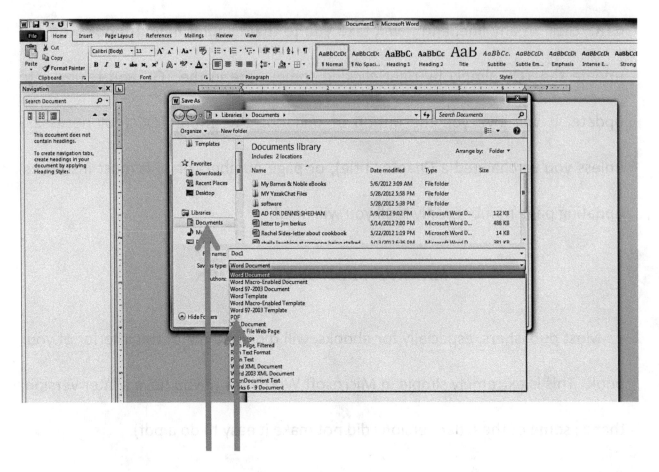

Next, click on "PDF" (right arrow)

Before you click "OK", make sure you have named your document and put it where you want it to be (left arrow)

NOW YOU ARE READY TO SUBMIT – GOOD LUCK!!

To purchase a copy of this book:
https://www.createspace.com/3891473
To see other works by Karen:
www.writingsbykaren.yolasite.com